Raising Student Aspirations

Classroom Activities
for Grades K-5

Russell J. Quaglia and Kristine M. Fox

CONFIDENCE to TAKE ACTION

LEADERSHIP and RESPONSIBILITY

SPIRIT of ADVENTURE

CURIOSITY and CREATIVITY

FUN and EXCITEMENT

SENSE of ACCOMPLISHMENT

HEROES

BELONGING

Research Press 2612 North Mattis Avenue • Champaign, Illinois 61822 • [800] 519-2707 • www.researchpress.com

Composition by Jeff Helgesen
Cover design by Linda Brown, Positive I.D. Graphic Design, Inc.
Printed by McNaughton & Gunn, Inc.

ISBN 0-87822-480-7
Library of Congress Catalog Number 2002095758

Contents

Chapter 8: Confidence to Take Action

Foreword

Russ Quaglia is an educator with an unusual mission. He wants children not only to be successful in school but to have fun doing it. As the founder and director of the Global Institute for Student Aspirations, he has earned a wide and enviable reputation as a champion of student motivation.

In numerous books, articles, presentations, and TV appearances, Russ has laid out his deceptively simple formula for getting elementary school children to achieve their full potential. It is a formula based on solid research and shaped by eight interrelated conditions: Belonging, Heroes, Sense of Accomplishment, Fun and Excitement, Curiosity and Creativity, Spirit of Adventure, Leadership and Responsibility, and Confidence to Take Action.

You will find each of these conditions highlighted in this book. Russ and co-author Kristine Fox have provided classroom teachers with a rich variety of activities designed to lay a foundation for student aspirations, and then provide the motivation to make aspirations a way of life.

Although it's a book that was written specifically for teachers, there is rich food for thought here for school administrators. Speaking for myself and the 29,500 members of the National Association of Elementary School Principals (NAESP), I see a seamless blending of Russ Quaglia's approach to building student aspirations and the creation of a school culture that embraces the whole child.

The principal's role as an instructional leader is not only to strive for success for all students, but to inspire them and make them feel part of a learning community. Principals accomplish this by training and encouraging teachers to imbue in their students the very qualities that Russ has consistently championed.

Look over the activities in this book and you will see why Russ's approach has been so successful. What child wouldn't have fun helping make a class quilt, playing word games, learning how to juggle, decorating the classroom, or making a secret code? They are all here, and each has a specific objective to Russ's mission to mold lifelong aspirations into the character of our students.

American education needs more visionaries like Russ Quaglia.

Vincent L. Ferrandino
Executive Director
National Association
of Elementary School Principals

Introduction

As a teacher, you have the opportunity to create wonderful learning environments for your students every day. You have the power to make school an exciting, creative, and engaging place where students want to learn. Schools that support, understand, and truly believe in the potential of all students are on their way to developing a culture that supports student aspirations. Promoting student aspirations means that, as a teacher, you are inspiring your students to reach their full potential.

We have identified eight conditions that need to be in place in order for aspirations to flourish. These conditions are fostered through classroom activities, interactions, discussions, and school-wide initiatives. The eight conditions are as follows:

1. Belonging

2. Heroes

3. Sense of Accomplishment

4. Fun and Excitement

5. Curiosity and Creativity

6. Spirit of Adventure

7. Leadership and Responsibility

8. Confidence to Take Action

The activities in this book are designed to help you understand and promote these eight conditions. Although the conditions are described and meant to be introduced in your classroom in a set order, they also fit into three distinct categories.

Three Conditions That Serve as the Foundation for Raising Student Aspirations

The first condition is *belonging.* Belonging activities focus on helping students feel valued for their unique talents and interests. At the same time, these activities help to establish a community in your classroom. You should focus on establishing the condition of belonging the minute students enter the building on the first day of school. You should then continually support and reinforce this condition throughout the school year.

The second condition, *heroes,* focuses on helping students find at least one adult they can trust and turn to for advice. This adult serves as a hero by connecting with the student and promoting the student's desire to connect with others as well. Hero activities help students discover who the real heroes are in their lives, as well as understand that they, too, are heroes. Students who have high aspirations also have real heroes in their lives—people they can turn to for advice, support, and guidance.

The third condition, *sense of accomplishment,* promotes effort, perseverance, and good citizenship. Although academic achievement is critically important to students, there is more to learning than making the grade. Sense of accomplishment activities encourage students to put forth effort and persevere so that they will be successful in life as they mature into responsible citizens.

Three Conditions That Motivate Students and Instill Enthusiasm in the Classroom

The fourth condition is *fun and excitement.* Like the next two conditions, it focuses on the importance of making learning engaging for all students. Fun and excitement activities concentrate on helping students to enjoy school by teaching them to laugh while they learn. You will notice that students who find school exciting will also be engaged and interested in the learning process. They will feel motivated and enthusiastic about what you are teaching them.

The fifth condition, *curiosity and creativity,* is notable not only because it allows students to question and explore what they are learning, but also because it encourages them to remain inquisitive both inside and outside the classroom.

The sixth condition, *spirit of adventure,* has to do with your supporting students to take healthy risks, set goals for themselves, and not worry about failing. Activities that promote spirit of adventure encourage students to set high, achievable goals. Although students may fail in their first few attempts to take healthy risks and set meaningful goals, they can—with your help—learn to keep trying. By persevering, they will have captured the essence of the condition of spirit of adventure.

Two Conditions That Establish the Mind-Set Students Need in Order to Aspire

The seventh condition, *leadership and responsibility,* involves giving every student a voice in the learning environment. Leadership and responsibility activities teach students to be leaders and to work with others. All students have the potential to be leaders and to cooperate with those around them. What they need from you is your desire to teach them the necessary skills and to support them as they develop their unique leadership styles. With your help, they will acquire the mind-set they need in order to aspire.

The eighth condition, *confidence to take action,* relies on your encouraging students to believe in themselves and their abilities. Activities that promote confidence to take action support the development of your students' self-image and also acknowledge their special talents and wonderful contributions to your class, your school, and the world at large.

How the Eight Conditions Benefit Everyone

Supporting student aspirations in the classroom is both exciting and rewarding. As a teacher, you need to understand that promoting aspirations is not the same as implementing an add-on unit or a special program; rather, it is a way of thinking. Fostering aspirations in the classroom is about believing that all students deserve to be acknowledged, understood, cared about, and supported in all their wonderful endeavors.

The activities presented in this book are meant to enhance what great teachers do every day. Great teachers engage their students, have a passion for teaching and learning, and truly love the teaching profession. Keep in mind that these activities should be used to complement a school culture that already promotes and supports the development of student aspirations. It is hoped that these activities will help students and staff better understand the eight conditions that affect the development of their own aspirations.

The introduction of these activities in the classroom is a great way to begin raising student aspirations. Ideally, you, the teacher, should participate in these activities, too. Most of the activities can be done at any point in the school year, can be adapted for a variety of grade levels, and can be modified to suit the unique nature of your classroom. For example, when younger students are not able to participate in writing exercises, these activities can be conducted as classroom discussions.

We are well aware of the constant time pressures teachers face every day. We also know that investing time and energy in promoting student aspirations will have a positive effect on you, your students, and everyone in your school. These activities will breathe new life into your classroom and create an exciting learning environment. We hope you have fun with them as you help student aspirations flourish.

CHAPTER ONE

BELONGING

CONFIDENCE to TAKE ACTION

LEADERSHIP and RESPONSIBILITY

SPIRIT of ADVENTURE

CURIOSITY and CREATIVITY

FUN and EXCITEMENT

SENSE of ACCOMPLISHMENT

HEROES

BELONGING

ACTIVITY 1   Individuality

One way to help your students understand that their unique talents and personalities are an important part of your class is to create a class quilt. This activity, which can be adapted for all grade levels, helps students understand that we all have a need to belong to a group or organization and that the classroom should be a place where everyone belongs.

Materials
- ▶ Quilt squares made from paper or cloth
- ▶ Pencils or small, thin paintbrushes
- ▶ Glue or tape, or a needle and thread

Instructions
1. Explain to the class that they are going to create a class quilt. To help the students visualize the quilt, you may want to show them samples of quilts or even discuss the history of quilts.
2. Give each student a square of paper that he or she can glue or tape to another square of paper or a swatch of cloth sturdy enough to be sewn to another piece of fabric.
3. Depending on the time and materials available, have the class draw, sew, or paint something about themselves on their quilt squares. Be sure to provide them with a central theme, such as Unique Talents or Special Interests.
4. Once the quilt has been completed, make sure it is displayed where everyone in the class can see it and enjoy it.

Discussion
1. What do we each bring as individuals to this class?
2. How do all of our unique talents and interests make this a better class?
3. How can we as a class help students belong who do not feel that they belong?

Enrichment
Explore the history of quilts and what they meant—and mean—to the people sewing them.

Have the entire school create one quilt. Hang the quilt in the entranceway to the school or at a community site, such as the library. Encourage students to make family quilts.

Watch Us Grow

This activity involves planting a garden—an exciting project that can teach students a lot about belonging. During the planting process, draw the students in by discussing with them the many different varieties of trees, plants, flowers, and other vegetation that exist. Emphasize how boring the garden or forest would be if it consisted of only one species, as well as how low the garden's survival rate would be in such a case. Assure the students that each of their seeds is going to be planted to help grow one beautiful garden.

Materials
- ▶ Flowerpots
- ▶ Flower or vegetable seeds and potting soil
- ▶ Decorating materials

Instructions
1. Distribute flower or vegetable seeds to the students.
2. Give students a flowerpot and decorating material and ask them to paint and decorate the flowerpot. (If you have difficulty finding flowerpots, you may wish to use the disposable plastic pots available from nurseries or ask for some from families at the beginning of the planting season.)
3. Have students sow the seeds and nurture their plants in the classroom until they are ready to be moved outside.
4. As a class, decide first where the garden will be and then make a design for the garden.
5. Have your students plant the flowers and enjoy the beauty the class created together.

Discussion
1. In what ways are your plants alike? How are they different? What is something that is true about all plants?
2. How are people alike or different? What are some characteristics that all people share?
3. How did we have to work together to create our garden?

Enrichment
Have students explore the importance of ecosystems to various cultures.

Ask students to ponder how environments are reflections of the people who live there.

ACTIVITY 3   Fun with Words

You may want to try this activity after a short discussion about belonging. It should help your class understand the importance of accepting students for who they are, as well as how significant each of them is as a unique individual.

Materials
- ▶ Belonging Worksheet
- ▶ Pencils or pens

Instructions
1. Give your students the Belonging Worksheet.
2. Challenge the students to write down one phrase or sentence per letter that not only begins with the letter but also relates to the condition of belonging. For example, for the letter *B,* a student's response might read, "Being there when my friend needs me makes me feel good."
3. Be sure to allow time for students to share their responses with the rest of the class.
4. If you feel that some or all of your students may have difficulty writing responses to complete this activity, engage them in a classroom discussion and encourage them to verbalize their thoughts.

Discussion
1. Why is the idea of belonging so important?
2. Can you recall a time when you did not fit in? What did it feel like?
3. How can we help all students feel that they belong?

Enrichment
Take the time to discuss words and the impact they have on people. For instance, how does a simple word like *stupid* make someone feel?

What are some words that are inclusive and promote the condition of belonging?

What are some words we use that are not welcoming to one another?

Belonging Worksheet

B _____

E _____

L _____

O _____

N _____

G _____

I _____

N _____

G _____

Raising Student Aspirations: Classroom Activities for Grades K–5
© 2003 by Russell J. Quaglia and Kristine M. Fox. Champaign, IL: Research Press (800) 519-2707

Our Class

The purpose of this activity is to help your class understand how important it is for all students to feel that they belong to their classroom community. It is a great activity to perform at the beginning of the school year because, from the outset, it helps establish a class identity.

Materials
▶ A sheet of construction paper and pencils or crayons
▶ String

Instructions
1. Together with the students, come up with a name for your classroom and write it on the sheet of construction paper. Use the string to hang the piece of paper on the classroom door.
2. Have the class create a song, class colors, or anything else that is special to them.
3. Brainstorming with your students, develop classroom rules and consequences.
4. Throughout the year, develop new class ideas, some of which may involve the class in community service projects.

Discussion
1. Why is it difficult to make group decisions?
2. How can we respect one another's answers even if we do not all agree?
3. What makes our class a special place to be?

Enrichment
Have students create several school songs or phrases. Ask the entire student body to vote on which ones they want to use for the school year.

Encourage your students to create family crests and logos at home.

Welcome to Our School

Younger students whose families move to a new location often discuss how difficult it is to enroll in a new school and how they just don't feel a sense of belonging. This activity helps students take ownership of their school and teaches them how to welcome new students to the school. It can be done every year and at all grade levels.

Materials

▶ Loose-leaf writing paper and pencils or pens

▶ A loose-leaf notebook

Instructions

1. As a class, use the loose-leaf paper and notebook to develop a handbook and protocol for new students. The handbook should be written by the students and consist of information helpful to all students. For example, it can be used to explain the cafeteria rules and the games kids play at recess.

2. After the handbook has been completed, discuss how your class will welcome new students. This welcome might include a building tour; a fun, get-to-know-you activity; or anything else the students might think of that would help new students feel comfortable at the school.

3. As new students become veterans, solicit their input and ideas for the handbook.

4. If your students are uncomfortable with their writing skills, you can solicit their ideas during a class discussion and then do the actual writing in the handbook yourself.

Discussion

1. What does it feel like to be a new student?

2. What does it feel like to leave your friends at your old school?

3. How can we be extra-friendly to new students?

Enrichment

Present the handbook to various school groups, including the school board and parent organizations.

Keep in mind that students may also want to illustrate the book and create a new student Web site.

ACTIVITY 6   Birthday Buddies

This activity helps establish a sense of belonging in the classroom by having the class post each student's birthday on homemade bulletin boards. Encourage your students to be as creative as possible when constructing these boards. Remember to post your own and perhaps other teachers' birthdays on the bulletin boards.

Materials
- ▶ Drawing paper and pencils and markers
- ▶ Material to make bulletin boards
- ▶ Tape and glue

Instructions
1. Each month, allow students to create a bulletin board that is to be used to notify everyone of student and staff birthdays for that particular month.

2. Make sure that students are grouped according to birth month, with each group choosing a symbol for that month. For example, students whose birthdays fall in October may want to choose autumn-colored leaves as their symbol.

3. Have students write their names and birthdays on the symbol their group created and then glue or paste the symbol to the bulletin board.

4. Each month, have students whose birthday month it is produce their own personal birthday bulletin boards and decorate them with their symbols. Encourage students to be creative.

Discussion
1. What are different ways people celebrate birthdays?
2. How does celebrating your birthday make you feel special?
3. Who else outside of this class shares your birthday?

Enrichment
Read stories to your class that describe how other cultures celebrate birthdays. Discuss with your students similarities and differences among cultures.

ACTIVITY 7   **Interesting Facts**

The purpose of this activity is to allow students time to discover heretofore unknown facts about their classmates. Students will find it entertaining to learn interesting things about their classmates.

Materials
► Interesting Facts Worksheet
► Pencils or pens

Instructions
1. Give each student a copy of the Interesting Facts Worksheet.
2. Have the students pass their worksheets to different classmates to see which of them can identify with any of the completed sentences. Those students who can should then write their name in the appropriate space (next to the interesting fact that applies to them). Students are permitted to sign their name only once on a classmate's worksheet.
3. Have students share what they learned about each other.

Discussion
1. How can everyone's individual talents benefit us as a class?
2. What are some talents we have in common?
3. What surprised you about one of your classmates?

Enrichment
Ask students to create their own talent worksheet questions without the help of the teacher.

Instruct students to write a biography of one of their classmates.

Interesting Facts Worksheet

Find someone in our class who . . .

1. . . . plays a band instrument.   Student: _____

2. . . . gets good grades in math.   Student: _____

3. . . . has a unique pet.   Student: _____

4. . . . spent summer vacation
   many miles away.   Student: _____

5. . . . has a good singing voice.   Student: _____

6. . . . has met a well-known
   or famous person.   Student: _____

7. . . . is an excellent speller.   Student: _____

8. . . . wants to become a baseball player.   Student: _____

9. . . . earns money after school
   by mowing lawns.   Student: _____

10. . . . (Complete a sentence of your own.)   Student: _____

_____

_____

Raising Student Aspirations: Classroom Activities for Grades K–5
© 2003 by Russell J. Quaglia and Kristine M. Fox. Champaign, IL: Research Press (800) 519-2707

It is important for all students to feel that they are a significant part of the classroom. For this reason, classroom rules and the utilization of classroom space should be decided with the help of student input. This activity helps personalize the use of classroom space throughout the entire school year.

Materials
▶ Yarn or long strips of paper

▶ Tape

▶ Student work, pictures, or any other materials students wish to post

Instructions
1. Designate one classroom wall the student wall.

2. Using yarn or long strips of paper, help the students divide the wall into as many squares as there are students. Use tape to affix the yarn or paper to the wall.

3. Assign each student a square in which to post schoolwork, pictures, or anything else that fits the allotted space. Remind students to change their postings at least twice a month.

Discussion
1. What have you learned about your classmates?

2. How did you decide what to put in your square?

3. How do we make a classroom feel as if it is ours?

Enrichment
Allow students the opportunity to create hallway displays or front entranceway displays. In creating the exhibit, students may want to work together with another class or with younger students.

Challenge Activities for Belonging

For Students
- ► Challenge your students to sit with someone different at lunch each day for a week. This task will be a real challenge for many students, but the rewards are great.
- ► Ask your students to invite someone to play with their recess group who usually does not play with them.
- ► Give your students the opportunity to brainstorm ways to make your class and the school more welcoming and accepting.

For Teachers
- ► Take the time to learn something new about each of your students. Use this information when developing and teaching lessons.
- ► Spend time with a colleague in your building with whom you usually do not interact on a regular basis.
- ► Share one of your hobbies or interests with your students.
- ► Attend your students' extracurricular activities.

CHAPTER TWO

HEROES

CONFIDENCE to TAKE ACTION

LEADERSHIP and RESPONSIBILITY

SPIRIT of ADVENTURE

CURIOSITY and CREATIVITY

FUN and EXCITEMENT

SENSE of ACCOMPLISHMENT

HEROES

BELONGING

| ACTIVITY 1 | **My Hero** | |

Students often do not realize that they have real heroes in their lives. These heroes are people who care about students' success and hold high expectations for them. This activity helps students realize that people all around them are willing to listen to them and accept them for who they are.

Materials
▶ 5 sheets of loose-leaf paper per student
▶ A loose-leaf notebook
▶ Pencils and coloring supplies

Instructions
1. Hand out the paper and pencils to the students and ask them to think of five important people in their lives. Ask them to list one person per sheet of paper.

2. Have the students accompany each person's name with a drawing or other rendering that is representative of the person. For example, students may list relatives who are important to them because they love animals. In that case, they may want to embellish one or more sheets of paper with drawings of animals.

3. Ask the students also to list on each page five reasons each person is important to them.

4. Collect the students' papers and insert them in the loose-leaf notebook, which you will refer to as the Hero Book.

5. Display the Hero Book prominently so the students can share one another's work.

Discussion
1. What traits do most of our heroes have in common?
2. Who are you a hero to?
3. How can we be better heroes to one another in this class?

Enrichment
Ask the students to write about a hero in their community.

Remind your students that heroes do not have to be rich or famous or well known.

Send copies of the hero stories to the heroes themselves.

We All Are Heroes

Students often think of heroes as those people whose names appear on TV or in the newspaper because of wonderful, heroic acts they have performed. This activity helps students understand that they, too, can be heroes—that they can make a difference in someone's life by performing simple acts of kindness.

Materials
► A shoe box
► Slips of paper and pencils or pens

Instructions
1. Tell the class that you would like to recognize students who perform helpful acts.
2. Take a few minutes to brainstorm a list of examples of such acts so that students understand how they can be helpful in the classroom and in the school.
3. Explain to the students that (using the shoe box) you have created a Hero Box and that you have placed a supply of slips of paper outside the box.
4. Tell the students that, once a week, they should put in the box the name of one student written on a slip of paper, along with an explanation of why that student was a hero.
5. At the end of each week, take the time to read a few of the slips aloud. Acknowledge other slips by writing your students a brief note of appreciation.
6. Invite guests into your classroom to hear about the various heroic acts your students are performing every week.

Discussion
1. How difficult was it to find acts of kindness being performed throughout the school?
2. What does it feel like to know that your classmates are doing great things?
3. How does it feel to be considered a hero?

Enrichment
Ask students to keep a hero log. In the log they should write about heroic things they see other students doing. They should also explain why they consider these acts heroic.

ACTIVITY 3   Hero Search

This activity introduces students to wonderful, touching stories about heroes that are worth reading to and with your students. These stories may include people who overcame incredible odds to achieve something or people who risk their lives for others every day. You may even find stories about people from your own community. The more real-life, the better.

Materials
- ▶ Reading list of books pertaining to heroes
- ▶ Books about these heroes that students can borrow from the school library

Instructions
1. Compile a reading list for students that includes stories about heroes. Make sure the stories vary in their nature and scope.
2. Ask students to choose a story to read.
3. Have students then share the story they chose and explain why they consider the subject of the story a hero.
4. As teacher, it is important for you also to share a favorite hero story.

Discussion
1. Why do you consider the main character a hero?
2. How did the character become a hero?
3. What other heroes do you know about?

Enrichment
Invite community leaders into your classroom to share their own life stories. Before doing so, take the time to prepare a list of questions students can ask about what constitutes a hero. Vary the kinds of people you invite to your class.

ACTIVITY 4   **Be a Hero**

Older students have an amazing ability to influence younger students in a positive, meaningful way. As a matter of course, younger students look up to and emulate their older, more experienced counterparts. As this activity emphasizes, it is important for students to understand how they are looked up to and what it means to be someone's role model.

Materials ▶ Writing paper and pencils or pens

Instructions

1. Once a week, pair up older and younger students at recess or lunchtime, during reading time, or whenever it works best in your building. Be sure to pair up the older students with students who are at least three grades behind them.

2. Discuss with the older students what it means to be a positive role model. Have them explain what they consider to be appropriate conversations and activities to engage in with younger students.

3. Encourage the older students to be creative when they are paired up with the younger students. Toward this end, allow the older students time to plan activities, write them down on paper, and discuss them with you.

Discussion

1. Why is it important to be a positive role model?

2. How do you show someone that you are actively listening?

3. How can you be a mentor to younger students every day?

Enrichment

Allow your older students to organize recess games for the younger students. Or perhaps a few older students at a time can eat lunch with the younger students several times a month.

Find older students to be mentors to your younger students. Make sure the older students receive training and support before they begin mentoring.

Who Am I?

Giving students the opportunity to share their unique skills and talents is a great way for classmates to learn to appreciate one another. As this activity shows, students often forge new friendships when they find a skill or talent they have in common.

Materials
▶ None

Instructions
1. Let your students know that they are going to take part in a creative show-and-tell.

2. The show-and-tell involves students' sharing something about themselves, with the emphasis placed on their sharing a specific talent or skill. (In some cases, you may need to help students think of ways to share the things they do really well.)

3. Give the students time to ask questions of each other.

4. Let students highlight their skills in class and also during open house and other schoolwide events.

Discussion
1. What new talent or skill would you like to learn?

2. What else would you like to know about one of your classmates?

3. How did you develop your special talents?

Enrichment
Encourage your students to develop new hobbies or skills. Have them think about what they are interested in and then search for ways to improve their skills. For example, some students may be interested in music. If so, how do they plan to pursue that hobby?

Provide the class with a list of creative and unique hobbies and skills.

ACTIVITY 6   Positive Traits

Heroes are all around us. Because there are no specific guidelines for being a hero, heroes possess a wide variety of characteristics and talents. As for those students who are seeking heroes, one may need a hero who is fun, whereas another may need a hero who is patient and kind. This activity helps students to see the diverse traits that heroes possess.

Materials
▶ Positive Traits Worksheet
▶ Extra-large sheets of butcher paper (large enough for students to lie down on)
▶ Markers and pencils or pens

Instructions
1. Give each student a copy of the Positive Traits Worksheet.
2. Ask students to list on the sheet five positive traits they have and five positive traits they look for in someone who is important to them. (If you use the word *hero,* rather than the term *someone important,* students often think only of those people deemed "heroes" by the media.)
3. Pair up students and give them extra-large sheets of butcher paper and a marker. Have the partners uses the marker to trace around each other's body.
4. Ask students to write their positive traits on the paper, inside the outline of their body. Then have them write, outside the outline of their body, the positive traits of the person who is important to them.
5. Give students the opportunity to decorate their body by drawing on the paper with the marker.
6. Discuss each student's drawing and display the class's hero bodies.

Discussion
1. How are our traits alike? How are they different?
2. What traits would you like to have that you did not write inside the outline of your body?
3. What trait do you feel is the most important for a hero to have?

Enrichment
Ask students to write about the people they admire. What traits do these people have? Do your students share any similar traits? How can they develop heroic traits every day?

Positive Traits Worksheet

My five most positive traits

1. _____

2. _____

3. _____

4. _____

5. _____

Five positive traits I look for in someone important to me

1. _____

2. _____

3. _____

4. _____

5. _____

Sometimes the most important heroes for students are right in front of their eyes; they simply go unnoticed. A hero may be the neighbor who says hello every day or the crossing guard who asks how an assignment went. Local heroes are highlighted in the paper all the time, but we often do not acknowledge them.

Materials
▶ Local newspapers or other publications
▶ Material to make a bulletin board

Instructions
1. Together with your students, create a bulletin board (referred to as a Hero Board) that highlights local heroes.
2. On a weekly basis, give your students the opportunity to scour the local paper or other area publications for stories about heroes.
3. Post the articles and pictures on your class Hero Board.
4. Invite local heroes in to speak with your class.

Discussion
1. How difficult was it to find local heroes?
2. What is something heroic you have done?
3. How can we all be better heroes at school?

Enrichment
Give students the opportunity to interview and meet local heroes. For instance, arrange a trip to the police station, firehouse, nursing home, or anyplace where there are enough people for everyone in your class to interview. Help students prepare their interview questions ahead of time.

Once back in class, add the text of the interviews and any accompanying pictures to your Hero Board.

Community Needs

Often we are unaware of many of our own community's needs. Students, it seems, are more likely to hear about national organizations and international relief efforts than about local goodwill campaigns. Perhaps that is the reason many classes tend to participate in fund-raising drives and charity events for people and organizations nationwide and worldwide. This activity focuses the students' attention on local concerns.

Materials

▶ Writing paper and pencils or pens

Instructions

1. Together with your class, develop a list of town or community needs. The organizations with these needs may range from a food pantry that needs volunteers, to the local park, which needs its equipment painted.

2. Decide upon one cause to help and agree to follow through with the project for the entire school year.

3. Create a plan of action. This plan may include writing letters to the appropriate people, inviting in guest speakers, and gathering materials.

4. Go do it! Make a difference in the community by being action oriented.

Discussion

1. What does it feel like to help others?

2. How are we heroes when we help out in our community?

3. How do you see other people helping in our community?

Enrichment

Encourage students to get their families involved in your class cause. You may even want to serve as host of a family get-together some evening as a way to involve parents.

Help your students write about their experiences as volunteers.

Challenge Activities for Heroes

For Students

▶ Have students write a thank-you note to someone who has made a difference in their life and let that person know that they consider him or her their hero.

▶ Have students take the time to get to know an elderly person in their neighborhood. Encourage them to arrange with their parents to visit and socialize with this person.

▶ Urge students to be a hero to their classmates by taking the time to help someone with homework or inviting a new student to play at recess with them.

For Teachers

▶ Develop a teacher-to-teacher mentoring program for new teachers.

▶ Create a community mentoring program in which community members work with students in your class. Make sure to provide training and support for the community mentors.

▶ Write a thank-you note to someone who has helped you professionally. It should be someone who has steadfastly believed in you and your abilities. Let the person know how much the help meant to you.

CHAPTER THREE
SENSE of ACCOMPLISHMENT

CONFIDENCE to TAKE ACTION

LEADERSHIP and RESPONSIBILITY

SPIRIT of ADVENTURE

CURIOSITY and CREATIVITY

FUN and EXCITEMENT

SENSE of ACCOMPLISHMENT

HEROES

BELONGING

ACTIVITY 1	**Learn a Trick**

It is important for students to experience the rewards of effort and hard work. This experience can occur in a variety of settings. The following activity allows students to have fun mastering a new skill. It may take practice, but the skill is accomplishable.

Materials
- ▶ Frisbees, jacks, balls, a jump rope
- ▶ Items that can be juggled
- ▶ Other sports equipment, as needed

Instructions
1. Explain to your students that with a bit of effort they are going to have the opportunity to master a new skill.

2. Set up a variety of stations, ideally in the gym or outside the building. Each station should be a place where students can perform a certain task and improve their skill. Tasks include, for example, playing jacks, throwing Frisbees, jumping rope, juggling, and hitting a target by kicking or throwing a ball.

3. Ask students to pick their two best activities and then tell them they are no longer allowed to choose the stations that feature those activities.

4. Give students enough time at each station so that they feel they have accomplished the task.

5. Take the time to do this type of activity several times during the school year.

Discussion
1. What did it feel like to get better at your activity?

2. How did you push yourself to succeed even when it was frustrating?

3. Can you name one task in particular that was especially difficult to perform?

Enrichment
Give students the opportunity to demonstrate their new skills. Challenge students to learn new skills outside of school and then allow them to share these with the class.

Give students several academic challenges to choose from each week. For example, one challenge may be to learn five difficult spelling words; another may be to create an art project that illustrates one of their assignments.

ACTIVITY 2   Share Your Achievements

Most schools do a good job of acknowledging students' academic and athletic achievements. However, many schools seem to overlook the wonderful accomplishments by students that occur outside of school. They tend not to notice that students who may not shine academically or athletically often have many other talents that go unrecognized. This activity helps to recognize such students.

Materials ▸ None

Instructions
1. Let your students know that, once a week, you will give a few students the opportunity to share an accomplishment they are proud of achieving.
2. Make sure to discuss the many ways people achieve.
3. Share with the class a unique accomplishment of your own.
4. Remember that this activity is not a show-and-tell. Rather, its purpose is to have students share something they have achieved.

Discussion
1. What are you proudest of achieving this year?
2. What would you like to achieve next year?
3. Why is it sometimes difficult to reach goals?

Enrichment
Give students the opportunity to chart their progress as they work on a yearlong goal. If they want to do better in an academic subject, help them create in their mind a visual reminder of this goal. If they choose a nonacademic goal, help them find a way to measure their progress.

ACTIVITY 3   Local Issue

Helping students understand that they have a voice in their community is an important component in the development of good citizenship. Students' voices are all too often forgotten or brushed aside when community or school decisions are being made. This activity helps students' voices to be heard.

Materials

► The local newspaper
► The school newspaper
► Stationery and pencils or pens

Instructions

1. Together with your students, decide on an important community or school issue you would like to tackle. For example, maybe the school is developing a new discipline code or the community is thinking about adding an after-school sports program.

2. Gather as much information as possible about the issue.

3. Develop a plan for students' voices and ideas to be heard. This plan may include writing letters, attending meetings, or sending students' ideas to the appropriate person.

4. As their teacher, you will have to do whatever is necessary to be viewed as a strong student advocate. By doing so, you will ensure that they are taken seriously.

5. Review the students' progress and accomplishments on a regular basis.

6. If you find that this activity is too difficult for youngsters this age, encourage them to discuss with you and the rest of the class their views on the local issue at hand. Modify the activity, but concentrate on ensuring that your students know their voices are being heard.

Discussion

1. Why do you think students often are not taken seriously when it comes to important issues?

2. Why is it important for students to get involved?

3. What does it feel like to have people listen to your ideas and then act upon them?

Enrichment

Once a month, give your students the opportunity to write their local or state representatives about an issue that concerns them. Make sure all letters are proofread and of the best quality. If the students are unable to perform this writing activity, then help them get their ideas across verbally and teach them the process involved in letter writing so that, in time, they will know how to contact their elected representatives.

We all want our students and children to be good citizens. Unfortunately, all too often schools provide only a few opportunities throughout the school year for students to practice good citizenship. Students need to understand the importance of being a good citizen every day and not just around the holidays. This activity should help get the point across.

Materials ▶ None

Instructions

1. Keeping in mind the age and maturity of your students, engage them in brainstorming possible yearlong citizenship projects that can be completed at school. Projects may involve such efforts as starting a recycling program, reading to younger students, or helping out at recess.

2. Discuss with the class what it means to be a good citizen. Talk about the students in your class who have been good citizens.

3. Allow all your students the opportunity to participate in the school service projects.

4. At the end of the year, make sure to celebrate the class's accomplishments.

Discussion

1. How does it feel to help others?

2. How are you a good citizen outside the school?

3. How can you be an even better citizen at school?

Enrichment

Invite local citizens who volunteer their time to stop by and speak with the class about what they do and why it is important to volunteer. Make sure the class thanks the volunteers for what they do in the community. The students may also want to share their citizenship projects with the volunteers who visit the classroom.

Great Accomplishments

Many wonderful inventions have been created through hard work, effort, and perseverance. Students, however, often don't have the opportunity to try, try, and try again on projects or assignments. This activity encourages students to keep improving.

Materials ▸ None

Instructions

1. Before beginning this activity, hold some discussions about inventions. Students will quickly chime in with what they feel is the neatest or most fascinating invention they've seen.

2. Ask students to think about how long it takes inventors to develop a new product. Remind them that people often fail many times before they succeed.

3. Depending on the grade level of your students, this activity can be done in one of two ways:

   Younger students

   Prepare a variety of easy science experiments. The gooey, edible ones are always fun.

   After the students do the experiment, ask them how they could make the experiment better, different, or more fun. Their ideas may include changing colors, adding steps, or throwing in a new ingredient.

   Point out to the students that there is always room for improvement and that they should always try to improve.

   Older students

   Ask older students to invent something on their own that they can make with everyday items. This undertaking will take time and planning. Encourage students to be creative, and remind them that before the automobile was invented, many people thought Henry Ford's ideas were crazy. Have the students try to imagine what people who lived in the early 1900s would have thought about computers or DVDs or CDs. Remind them that even most of the people living in the latter part of the 20th century could not have conceived of today's technological advances.

   After the students have come up with their inventions, give them the opportunity to try to improve them. Have them solicit ideas for improvement from classmates, parents, and teachers.

   Praise the students for their effort, perseverance, and creativity.

Discussion   1. Why was this activity challenging?

2. If you could invent one thing, what would it be?

3. What do you think is the best invention of all time?

Enrichment   Encourage students to keep a journal of inventions and ideas. Share stories of student inventions and emphasize to your students that, through effort and perseverance, anything is possible.

ACTIVITY 6   Effort Awards

Students are often recognized for academic, athletic, and artistic achievements. To honor these students, many schools hold monthly award assemblies at which a select group of individuals is recognized. But what about the students who try really hard but never seem to make the highest marks or design the best projects? As this activity shows, it is important to recognize that putting forth effort is a wonderful accomplishment that also should be awarded.

Materials
► Effort Certificate
► Writing paper and pencils or pens

Instructions
1. Explain to your students the importance of effort and why students who put forth effort should be recognized.
2. Ask students to list the various ways people try really hard at school.
3. Tell your students that they can nominate one student a week to receive an Effort Certificate. Included with each nomination must be an explanation of why the person deserves the award.
4. At the end of the week, consider all nominations and choose one student to be recognized and awarded an Effort Certificate.

Discussion
1. Why is it important to put forth effort?
2. What does it mean to persevere?
3. What task have you put forth the greatest effort in achieving?

Enrichment
Together with your students, create effort reports to be sent home to parents once a quarter. Students should be encouraged to self-evaluate and comment on areas in which they need to try harder.

Effort Certificate

This effort certificate, dated _____,

is hereby awarded to _____

for superior effort and perseverance

during the week of _____.

ACTIVITY 7   Caught You Doing Good!

We often forget how frequently students perform acts of kindness. Students are well known for helping each other out, inviting other kids to play with them, or just picking up trash around the school. This activity helps underscore the importance of recognizing these various displays of good citizenship.

Materials
- ► 5 slips of paper per student
- ► Pencils
- ► A shoe box
- ► Decorating materials

Instructions
1. Ask your students to think about the times they have seen other students in the school doing nice things. What nice things did the students do?
2. Tell your students that you would like to find a way to recognize students for doing nice things.
3. Each week, hand out five slips of paper to every student. On each slip, students should write down the name of a student they "caught doing something good," as well as the good deed done by the student. (Students should be encouraged to recognize the good deeds done by students who are not their friends.)
4. Instruct the students to drop their slips of paper in the shoe box, which has been designated the Caught You Doing Good Box. As teacher, you may also want to drop slips in the box to reward students for good citizenship.
5. If you'd like, ask for volunteers to decorate the box.
6. On the last day of every week, draw one name from the box. The student whose name is chosen should be applauded and receive a special prize.
7. It is a good idea to announce the winner of the drawing during the time of day that regular school announcements are made. Students will greatly anticipate these drawings.

Discussion
1. In what ways can we all be good citizens at school?
2. How do you see adults being helpful to others at school?
3. What can we do as a class to promote better citizenship?

Enrichment
Ask students to share their ideas about good citizenship and their experiences with good citizenship shown by younger students. Some students may want to perform a skit, whereas others may want to share artwork depicting good citizenship. Students should plan and practice their presentations.

Future Achievements

It's no secret that many students have difficulty planning for the next day, let alone the rest of the school year. This activity helps students begin to think about goal setting and what goals they want to achieve.

Materials
▶ Writing paper and pencils or pens
▶ A wall chart
▶ Tape
▶ Stars or stickers

Instructions
1. Engage your students in a discussion about goal setting. What types of goals do people set and why? Tell your students that together the class is going to set goals.

2. Ask your students to brainstorm class goals. These goals may include listening better, completing homework promptly, or getting to class on time.

3. Create a class goal for each week. Have the students think about how the class is going to achieve the goal and how they can help one another be successful.

4. Write the goal on the chart, then tape the chart to a classroom wall.

5. When students achieve a goal, place a star or a sticker on the chart.

6. Once the class has accumulated a specified number of stars, make sure you celebrate.

Discussion
1. What is difficult about goal setting?
2. Why do people set goals?
3. What personal goals do you have for this school year?

Enrichment
Have your students create personal goal books at least five pages thick. Ask them to think about goals they would like to achieve on their own.

Talk about how one achieves goals.

Allow students time both to share their goals with the class and to note their progress in their personal goal books.

Challenge Activities for Sense of Accomplishment

For Students
► Challenge students to promote good citizenship in their own neighborhoods. For example, have them find an elderly person who needs help with yard work and do it for free.

► Have students redo an assignment they know they can improve on, even if they are fairly sure their grade won't change.

► Encourage students to take the time to do volunteer work with a friend, parent, or sibling. Invite them to visit the local chamber of commerce so they can more readily come up with ideas about where they can volunteer.

For Teachers
► Model good citizenship for your students. Take the time to volunteer for an extra activity at school or in your community. Share your experiences with your students.

► Take a course in something that challenges you. If you are a social studies teacher, take a math course or math workshop. Learn something a little different.

► Make sure to recognize one student every day who simply tried extra-hard. Let the student know you recognized his or her effort and that you appreciate it.

CHAPTER FOUR

FUN and EXCITEMENT

CONFIDENCE to TAKE ACTION

LEADERSHIP and RESPONSIBILITY

SPIRIT of ADVENTURE

CURIOSITY and CREATIVITY

FUN and EXCITEMENT

SENSE of ACCOMPLISHMENT

HEROES

BELONGING

ACTIVITY 1   Our Room

Adding fun and excitement to our daily routines can be inspiring and motivational. It follows, then, that students who experience this condition throughout the school day are more likely to be engaged and involved in their own learning.

Materials
- ▶ Writing and drawing paper
- ▶ Crayons and regular and colored pencils
- ▶ Other classroom supplies for building models

Instructions
1. Inform your students that you would like their help with a decorating project.
2. Ask your students to think about their ideal classroom: How would the desks be arranged? Would there even be desks? What would the walls look like?
3. Give students the opportunity to draw, create a model, or write about their ideal classroom.
4. Allow students the opportunity to present their ideas to the class.
5. As a class, decide which ideas you can use and incorporate into your current class.

Discussion
1. What was difficult about this assignment?
2. What changes would you like to make in the appearance of the entire school?
3. How can we create fun and excitement every day in our class?

Enrichment
Give your students the opportunity to select classroom supplies. Make sure they are aware of the budget, and see to it that they are given plenty of catalogs to search for the items they want.

Teach for a week without desks in the classroom. Create alternative learning and working spaces for students.

Try often to make changes in the appearance of the classroom, and do so using student input.

Unit Titles

Have you ever wondered how students are supposed to get excited about unit titles such as Rocks or Sentence Fragments? Using this activity, you can spice up old units and textbooks by giving students the opportunity to create new unit titles. Students will welcome the opportunity to "help" the publishers by infusing fun and excitement into the title words.

Materials ▶ Current textbooks

Instructions
1. Inform your students that, for the benefit of future students, they are going to have the opportunity to create more interesting titles for the units they have read.

2. Be sure to remind the class that the new titles should sound enticing enough to attract students' interest and make them want to absorb the information that follows the titles.

3. Together with your students, brainstorm fun and exciting words: What do these words sound and look like?

4. Still working together with your students, select a typically mundane unit title that needs to sound more exciting. Let your students share their ideas freely.

5. At the end of each unit, give students the opportunity to rename it. Make sure, though, that the students have learned something about the subject matter before they rename the unit.

6. Because they are so young, your students may have difficulty thinking up new titles. To alleviate this problem, you may choose to write a variety of title suggestions on the chalkboard and have the students discuss the value of the words you have chosen.

Discussion
1. How does a title capture your interest?
2. What is your favorite book title? Why?
3. If you were to title your life, what title would you choose?

Enrichment
Hold a contest, instructing each student to come up with a new title for a particular unit and awarding a prize for the best title, as voted by the class.

Together with your students, send your title suggestions to the publisher of the text. Make sure you include a letter of explanation.

As a teacher, think about the words you choose to introduce a new lesson or unit. Is there a way to make the language more fun and exciting?

ACTIVITY 3　　　Laughter Is the Best Medicine

Who doesn't love to laugh? Think about how people's facial expressions and movements change when they have the opportunity to laugh and have fun. It is important for students to have that opportunity throughout the school day, to tell jokes or stories and just to laugh at times. This activity emphasizes the importance of laughter in the classroom.

Materials
- ► Joke books
- ► Comic strips or books

Instructions

1. Begin your teaching day by telling the students a joke. (Be prepared for the moans and groans!)

2. After your students have sufficiently protested your joke telling, turn the reins over to them.

3. Tell them that, throughout the day on Mondays, one student will be responsible for making others laugh. Each student should be assigned one Monday.

4. Every Monday, the student whose turn it is to make others laugh should come prepared with four or five jokes, cartoons, or comic strips. Throughout the day, allow the student to present his or her jokes, but within certain time limits. Use the jokes as a way to transition from one subject to another or as students are lining up to change classes or go to lunch.

Discussion

1. Why is it important to laugh?

2. What makes a joke funny?

3. How do you feel when you laugh?

Enrichment

Challenge students to think about jokes related to the subject they are studying. For example, if they are studying the atmosphere, what might be a joke one could tell about this subject?

Create a joke wall, where students can post and read each other's jokes and cartoons.

ACTIVITY 4   Mystery Balloons

Mysteries of any kind are a great way to bring about fun and excitement in the classroom. Mysteries provide suspense and almost always keep one wondering what is going to happen next.

Materials
► Balloons
► Slips of paper and pencils or pens

Instructions
1. This activity can be conducted in a number of ways. The basic method is for clues or assignments that have been written on slips of paper to be put inside balloons, which are then blown up.

   One way mystery balloons can be used is to choose the setting, place, and characters that make up a story. For example, you may have 10 balloons, and each balloon has a different character in it. Some students will pop a balloon and discover the name of the character they must write about. Other students will pop a balloon and find the central action in their story.

   Another fun way to use mystery balloons is for homework assignments. Before homework is assigned in math, for example, fill several mystery balloons with possible assignments. The assignments might range from differentiating odd numbers from even numbers or using addition and subtraction. You may even blow up one balloon that contains a slip of paper instructing the student who pops it that today is a homework holiday.

2. Be creative and have fun. This activity is sure to bring about excitement and will be remembered by your students years after they leave your class.

3. If you are concerned about the lack of writing skills of some of your students, encourage them to talk out their story, to verbalize their thoughts and share them with the rest of the class.

Discussion
1. What was fun about this activity?
2. How else can we make homework more fun?
3. What was your favorite homework assignment and why?

Enrichment
Create mysteries for your students to solve that revolve around their lessons. For example, one mystery may involve finding the misspelled words in an assignment or discovering the favorite foods of a character in a book. Or, if you are introducing a subject or project that allows students to feel, taste, or smell, make sure to use the opportunity as a mystery that must be solved.

| ACTIVITY 5 | **Dance Break** |

For most of a typical day, students are told to sit down, stay in line, or listen closely. Allowing students time for free expression will help open their minds and reenergize them for the rest of the day. This activity shows that students who are allowed physical movement grow mentally, improve their physical health, and have fun at the same time.

Materials
- A CD player
- A variety of music

Instructions
1. Begin by discussing with your students the type of music they like. You may even ask if anyone wants to sing a favorite song.
2. Let the students know that once a day they are going to have a 5-minute dance break.
3. Tell them you are going to play some music that they may or may not recognize.
4. Have the students dance to the music, but remind them to think about how someone would normally dance to the music being played. For example, one would not break-dance to classical music.
5. Make sure you play different types of music. Students will have fun dancing; at the same time, they will be increasing their exposure to different types of music.

Discussion
1. Why is music fun to listen to?
2. What makes a song popular?
3. What is your favorite type of music? Why?

Enrichment
Either take your students to a variety of dance performances or give them the opportunity to watch a dance on TV or on video. This approach will help introduce students to ballet or to dances that are either unique to our American heritage or specific to other ethnicities. They may even watch dance performances by the local high school students. If possible, invite a few high school students to teach your students new dance moves.

ACTIVITY 6   Word Searches

Word games and puzzles are great ways to help establish the condition of fun and excitement. As this activity shows, these games should be part of the curriculum.

Materials   ▶ A computer with access to the Internet

Instructions   1. Create games, word searches, or crossword puzzles for end-of-unit reviews for your students.

2. Locate on the computer a variety of Web sites that actually create puzzles if one inserts the necessary words or crossword clues. At the end of each unit, select an interesting game to help the students review their learning.

3. For those students who so desire, help create review games and puzzles.

Discussion   1. How can games help you learn?

2. What is your favorite game and why? (Use this information when developing your unit games.)

3. Do games have to be competitive to be fun? Explain.

Enrichment   Together with your students, create new games. The games may be those played at recess or review games the entire class can play. Students should help develop the rules, instructions, and the goals of the games. Students have fun with this challenge and are always excited when their game is used.

ACTIVITY 7　　　　3-D Structures

Whenever possible, students should be given opportunities to work with their hands and explore their artistic side. For many students, fun and excitement occur only when they have the opportunity to be creative, build, color, and generally explore their artistic talents. This activity helps students in this endeavor.

Materials　► A variety of building materials (e.g., Popsicle sticks, glue, paper, egg cartons, cardboard)

Instructions　1. Assign students the task of building a 3-D structure. The structure must have a purpose. The purpose may be useful or fictitious or just plain funny. For example, the structure may be something that holds all the used pencils, or it may be something whimsical (e.g., something that generates weather conditions).

2. You may want to develop specific guidelines for the class project. For example, you may require that the structure be strong enough not to fall apart when a pencil is dropped on it, that it be made out of only five different items, or that it be only a foot tall.

3. Pair up students and give them ample time to plan their project.

4. Give the students 30 minutes to build the best structure they can.

5. Have students present their project to the class. Make sure to allow them enough time to think about their presentation, for they should be able to describe their structure and explain its purpose and function.

6. This project may take several class periods to complete, depending on how detailed you want the structures to be.

Discussion　1. What challenges did you face in building your structures?

2. What could you have done differently to build a better structure?

3. What do you think is the biggest challenge builders face?

Enrichment　Through books or field trips, explore buildings and structures with your students. Introduce the students to various forms of architecture.

Give students the opportunity to draw and design a new school building from an architectural viewpoint.

Act It Out

Students of all ages love to dress up and get into character. As evidenced by this activity, the world of play and imagination is important for the development of fun and excitement.

Materials ▶ None

Instructions 1. Depending on the grade level of your students, this activity can be done every week in a variety of ways:

Younger students

When working with younger students, if the book of the week is about lions, allow students to roar like a lion, make manes, and strut around the room like a lion. If you are learning about the letter A, let students dress up so they represent words that begin with the letter A. For example, one student may dress as an avocado, whereas another may act like an ape. This visual reminder of the letter A is sure to help students remember the letter A.

Older students

If your students are older, challenge them to act out words, ideas, and concepts. For example, if the students are learning about weather patterns, how can these patterns be created through acting? What happens when hot air mixes with cold air? Or, if you are learning about the solar system and stars, how can this natural phenomenon be represented visually by the students?

2. Finding acting opportunities for your students may take a bit of creative planning; however, the reward will be lessons that your students remember for a long time.

Discussion 1. Why is it easy for some students to talk in front of people but difficult for others?

2. How can we help each other feel more comfortable speaking up in front of audiences?

3. What are a few important things to remember when performing in front of a group?

Enrichment Have everyone dress up as the characters your students are studying. Students will be eager to see what antics you will introduce in each new unit.

Challenge Activities for Fun and Excitement

For Students
- ► Give students the responsibility for creating a class bulletin board each month. The bulletin boards should be fun, exciting, and colorful.
- ► Give students the opportunity to rearrange desks and sit where they want, as long as they can follow class rules and guidelines.
- ► Once a month, let your students enjoy a potluck lunch. Everyone should have fun, listen to music, and play games during this period.

For Teachers
- ► Try teaching an old lesson a different way. Research the subject, talk with colleagues, and take a chance on teaching the subject a new and exciting way.
- ► Explore ways with your principal to make staff meetings more fun. Strive to have full staff engagement; make sure no one is grading papers or reading a magazine article.
- ► Add excitement to the teachers' room. Post jokes, cartoons, or words of wisdom on the walls. Put up lively posters and dare to paint the room a color that's not white or beige. Enlist the help of your colleagues to sponge-paint the room.

CHAPTER FIVE

CURIOSITY and CREATIVITY

CONFIDENCE to TAKE ACTION

LEADERSHIP and RESPONSIBILITY

SPIRIT of ADVENTURE

CURIOSITY and CREATIVITY

FUN and EXCITEMENT

SENSE of ACCOMPLISHMENT

HEROES

BELONGING

ACTIVITY 1   **What's That Called?**

Some students are naturally creative, whereas others need opportunities to help pique their creativity. Any activity that allows students to think a bit differently or take learning risks will promote the condition of curiosity and creativity. This activity is quite fun and can be used throughout the school year.

Materials   ▶ Writing paper and pencils or pens

Instructions

1. Tell students that you have noticed a lot of sounds and items that no one has bothered to name. Give a few examples, such as the sound a pencil sharpener makes or the word for the little pieces of paper that fall on the ground when you rip a page out of a spiral notebook.

2. Ask students to think of other sounds or items that have no name. Urge them to be creative.

3. Challenge students, individually or as a class, to create words for these nameless items. Make sure to keep track of these newly named items.

4. Whenever possible, use the new words. Your students will appreciate your remembering their words.

Discussion

1. How do items get their names (e.g., ketchup, desk, table)?

2. How difficult was it to think of new words? Why?

3. What everyday words do you think should be added to the dictionary?

Enrichment   Take the time to listen to all the words that are used on a daily basis that, according to the dictionary, actually are not words. Keep track of the slang, shortened, and made-up words that everyone in the school uses. Have the students search for these words in the dictionary. For those words that cannot be found, create a classroom slang dictionary.

ACTIVITY 2　　The Wrong Color

We all know that the sky is blue, the grass is green, and the sun is sometimes yellow or orange or red. But do these elements of nature really have to be these colors? The first challenge in promoting curiosity and creativity is to help students think for themselves and use their imagination. Students need to know that it is not only OK to paint a pink sky, but it is also encouraged.

Materials
- ► Painting supplies and an assortment of different-colored paints
- ► Drawing paper and pencils or pens

Instructions
1. This activity can be done two different ways: The first way is to give each student one color of paint, instruct the class to paint scenery, and encourage them to use their imagination and visualize things in a different way. (This activity will be a challenge for many students.)

2. Another way to do this activity is to give each student several colors of paint and instruct the class to paint scenery, with the caveat that they cannot use the colors one would typically use. Tell them, for example, that trees cannot be green and the sky cannot be blue; barns cannot be red and the ocean cannot be blue. (Again, this task will be a struggle for some students.)

3. Do some painting yourself and extend the boundaries of your creativity. Paint something upside down or sideways, or cut your drawing paper into a different shape. At the same time, model your creativity for your students so that they, too, can feel comfortable being outlandishly original.

Discussion
1. What was difficult about this activity?
2. Is it OK to see things differently?
3. Is there always a right way and a wrong way to complete a project? Explain.

Enrichment
Encourage students to be more creative with their writing and other projects. Create more open-ended assignments in which students have more choices and flexibility. Even try something as simple as giving students different sizes and shapes of paper to write on or different-colored pens and pencils.

ACTIVITY 3   I Wonder

Think about all the things there are to learn in this world. There are the typical facts, formulas, and rules, and then there are so many things that defy explanation. Have you ever tried to think about how something as simple as the phone works? The mere thought of sound traveling across oceans is quite impressive. This activity helps students explore all the creativity that is needed to be an inventor.

Materials
- ▶ I Wonder Worksheet
- ▶ Writing paper and pencils or pens

Instructions

1. Engage your students in a discussion about a number of history's amazing inventions. Make sure the examples are fairly simple to understand and can be explained to your students' satisfaction.

2. Ask students if they have ever wondered how something works. For example, have they ever wondered how music actually comes from a CD?

3. Give your students the I Wonder Worksheet and ask them to fill in the blanks, first listing the name of an invention and then asking a question about it. When the students have finished, collect all the worksheets.

4. Give your students one I Wonder question that is not their own and assign them the task of answering the question. The answer should be well thought out and creative but does not necessarily have to be correct. Make sure you give your students enough time to think seriously about their answers.

5. Share a few of the questions and answers with the class.

6. Once a week, share a creative but incorrect answer to a question and then follow up by sharing the correct answer. You may need to bring in guest speakers or other adults to help with some of the explanations.

Discussion

1. What did you learn from this activity that surprised you?

2. What do you think is the most amazing invention of all time? Why?

3. Is it more important to be correct or to be creative? Explain.

Enrichment

Use this same technique when you begin new lessons in class. For example, if you are studying frontier life, ask students to think of a few I Wonder questions. Students may say, for example, "I wonder what they did without TV" or "I wonder what they ate." Keep the I Wonder questions posted until they are answered.

I Wonder Worksheet

Name of invention

Question about the invention

1. _____

2. _____

3. _____

4. _____

5. _____

6. _____

7. _____

1. _____

   _____

2. _____

   _____

3. _____

   _____

4. _____

   _____

5. _____

   _____

6. _____

   _____

7. _____

   _____

Raising Student Aspirations: Classroom Activities for Grades K–5
© 2003 by Russell J. Quaglia and Kristine M. Fox. Champaign, IL: Research Press (800) 519-2707

Mystery Animal

Most everyone loves a mystery. Mysteries make you think, and they often do not turn out the way you thought they would. This activity shows how students can experience the fun of mysteries through stories, TV shows, and even pictures.

Materials
▶ Pictures of animals

▶ Construction paper and markers

▶ Tape or glue

Instructions
1. Inform students that you are going to present a mystery animal to the class once a week.

2. On the first day of the week, tape or glue a portion of a picture of the animal (e.g., a giraffe's leg) to the construction paper posted on the wall. In order to make the picture more of a mystery, you may need to use a photocopier to increase or decrease the size. Make sure the picture is not recognizable at first glance.

3. Allow students to submit one guess when they think they know the answer.

4. On day two, post one fact about the animal (e.g., the animal is native to Africa).

5. On day three, post another fact, and then keep posting facts until most of the students have the right answer. Let the student who first answers correctly choose the picture for the following week and help post the facts.

6. As the students get better at solving these mysteries, you may want to branch out from animals and even let the students oversee the entire mystery project.

Discussion
1. What do you like about mysteries?

2. What makes for a good mystery?

3. If you were to write a mystery, what would it be about?

Enrichment
Spend some time reading mysteries with your students. Encourage them to think about what will happen next in each story. You may even want them to write new endings to the mysteries or create their own mysteries.

What's the Ending?

Writing and drawing are wonderful ways to promote the condition of curiosity and creativity. Unfortunately, students often feel they have nothing to draw or nothing to write about. This activity helps students overcome their writer's block and their reluctance to draw and enables them to discover how wonderfully creative they can be.

Materials   ▶ What's the Ending? Worksheets

Instructions   1. Give each student a copy of both What's the Ending? Worksheets.

Story Starters

Have students expand on the four sentences provided on this worksheet.

Drawing Starters

Have students complete the unfinished pictures drawn on this worksheet.

2. Let the students know that the writer of each sentence just got writer's block and needs help completing the story. The writer wants creative, exciting, and dynamic events and characters. Give your students plenty of time to finish.

3. Let the students know that each artist just ran out of paint and needs help finishing the drawing. Give your students ample time to complete the drawings.

4. Encourage the students to share their creations with the rest of the class.

Discussion   1. Was this assignment easy or difficult? Explain.

2. What do you do when you have writer's block? How about when you have trouble completing a drawing?

3. How do you think authors think of new and exciting stories? How about artists and their drawings or paintings?

Enrichment   Give your students a variety of characters, settings, and scenes to work into their stories and drawings. You may even have them pick their characters, settings, and scenes out of a box. Students may end up with characters and scenes that do not seem to go together. Thus they will have to be creative.

What's the Ending? Worksheet

Story Starters

1. It was the last quarter of the state championship basketball game, and the score was still tied with only 10 seconds remaining.

   _____

   _____

   _____

2. As they walked to the library well past dark, Andre and Vern heard footsteps behind them, but they dared not turn around.

   _____

   _____

   _____

3. What started out as a harmless prank soon spiraled out of control.

   _____

   _____

   _____

4. Today the teacher told us we were going on a field trip next Friday.

   _____

   _____

   _____

© 2003 by Russell J. Quaglia and Kristine M. Fox. Champaign, IL: Research Press (800) 519-2707

What's the Ending? Worksheet

Drawing Starters

1.

2.

3.

4.

Students love to communicate using secret codes or invented languages. This activity encourages students to be creative and develop a new written language.

Materials   ▶ Secret Codes Worksheet

▶ Writing paper and pencils or pens

Instructions   1. Tell your students that they have been assigned the job of creating a new written language and will work in pairs to create symbols or signs for each letter of the alphabet. Give students the Secret Codes Worksheet, which provides examples of a partial master key, and invite them to make up their own symbols.

2. Have your students write a secret, coded message on a separate piece of paper. Students should trade messages and codes and try to decipher them.

3. You also should make up a secret code and give each student a key to your code. At the end of the week, send the kids home with a secret message they need to decipher over the weekend.

Discussion   1. Why are secret codes fun?

2. When do you think people use secret codes?

3. What other codes do you know?

Enrichment   This activity can also be done using math problems. In one such example, 4 actually equals *A,* and 1 actually equals *B.* Students must solve the math problems to get the answer and then translate the answer into a letter and a secret message. This is a fun and creative way to review for tests and do homework.

Secret Codes Worksheet

Partial Master Key:

       A = @

       B = #

       C = $ #*@% = BEAD

       D = %

       E = *

Your Own Master Key:

A = ____	**N** = ____
B = ____	**O** = ____
C = ____	**P** = ____
D = ____	**Q** = ____
E = ____	**R** = ____
F = ____	**S** = ____
G = ____	**T** = ____
H = ____	**U** = ____
I = ____	**V** = ____
J = ____	**W** = ____
K = ____	**X** = ____
L = ____	**Y** = ____
M = ____	**Z** = ____

Raising Student Aspirations: Classroom Activities for Grades K–5
© 2003 by Russell J. Quaglia and Kristine M. Fox. Champaign, IL: Research Press (800) 519-2707

| ACTIVITY 7 | **Nature Walk** |

Students of all ages love to get outside and explore their environments. We often walk by the same spot time after time and never really notice our environment. This activity encourages students to listen to the sounds outside their building.

Materials
► Writing paper and pencils or pens

Instructions
1. Tell your students that the class is going for a walk to listen to and observe their surroundings. Assign half the class the task of listening and the other half the task of observing. The half that is listening should just listen to all the sounds they hear and write them down. (Remind the students that they will have to be quiet for this activity to work.) You may want to enlist the help of another adult to take half the class in a different direction.

2. Encourage the listening group to branch out beyond the honk of a horn. Do they hear a cat meow in the distance or the rustle of leaves?

3. The observing group should be encouraged to observe the unusual, or things they normally do not notice. Do they see ants crawling in the grass or birds on the rooftops? Challenge the observers to list five observations that no one else has.

4. After your walk, bring the students back together to discuss their experiences.

Discussion
1. What was it like being quiet and outside?
2. What unusual things did you observe or hear?
3. What did you like about the silent time?

Enrichment
Do this same assignment in the cafeteria or at recess with a small group of students. Ask a few students at a time to observe and listen silently to their surroundings and then to report on their findings.

ACTIVITY 8   Color Collage

Art activities are another wonderful way to promote curiosity and creativity. This activity can produce some amazing projects and can be done at all grade levels.

Materials
- ▶ Drawing paper and an assortment of markers
- ▶ Magazines
- ▶ Glue
- ▶ Scissors

Instructions
1. Inform your students that they are going to create color collages. Each student must choose one color.
2. Have them cut out pictures displaying that color. For example, those who choose yellow might find pictures of the sun, a sunflower, or a yellow dress. (Some of this project can be completed at home.)
3. Once students have gathered enough pictures, they should create a collage of their color. Encourage students to be creative with their collages: Perhaps the paper can be cut in the shape of the sun for the color yellow or the shape of a cloud for the color white.
4. Make sure to display and share the students' artwork.

Discussion
1. What makes a color your favorite color?
2. What colors represent moods? Why?
3. What colors are associated with each season? Why?

Enrichment
Help students write an essay or short story about their color. What does yellow feel like, sound like, smell like? Why did they choose yellow? What does it remind them of?

Challenge Activities for Curiosity and Creativity

For Students
- ► Encourage your students to try something different in the classroom, such as sitting next to someone they usually don't sit next to, rather than sitting next to their best friend, or wearing slacks to school instead of blue jeans. Invite them to take a risk and be different.
- ► Tell students that the next time they don't know the answer to a question or don't know how something operates, they should ask someone who knows. The point is that they should not be afraid to ask questions and search for answers.
- ► Encourage students to create, draw, dance, sing, act, play music. Have them do something to get their creative juices flowing. Have them do something creative before sitting down to do their homework at night.

For Teachers
- ► Allow your students to sing, dance, perform, paint, draw, and express their creative side.
- ► Teach a lesson in a totally different way. Throw out your old lesson plan and be creative.
- ► Learn about a new subject that interests you. Share your new insights with your students.

CHAPTER SIX

SPIRIT of ADVENTURE

CONFIDENCE to TAKE ACTION

LEADERSHIP and RESPONSIBILITY

SPIRIT of ADVENTURE

CURIOSITY and CREATIVITY

FUN and EXCITEMENT

SENSE of ACCOMPLISHMENT

HEROES

BELONGING

ACTIVITY 1   No-Laughter Zone

One of the major obstacles to risk taking in the elementary school is students' fear of being laughed at. Many students find it easier and safer not to take a risk, even though the outcome may be rewarding. This activity helps students recognize that laughter is not always funny.

Materials
▶ Construction paper and markers
▶ Tape

Instructions

1. Inform students that the classroom is going to be a safe place to take risks. Point out to them that one way to make the classroom "safe" is not to laugh at one another.

2. Ask your students to share experiences they have had being laughed at for something they thought was not funny. You may want to help the students along by sharing a personal story.

3. Let students know that it is OK and fun to laugh, as long as someone's feelings are not hurt.

4. Ask each student to create a No-Laughter poster. Examples: "Don't laugh at me when I make a mistake." "Don't laugh at me when I miss the ball in baseball."

5. Tape the No-Laughter posters to the walls of the classroom and refer to them when necessary.

Discussion

1. What does it feel like to be laughed at?

2. Why is it funny when someone makes a mistake?

3. How can we be more supportive of one another in this class?

Enrichment

Play the Peter, Paul, and Mary song "Don't Laugh at Me." Ask your students to think about the song and then discuss it.

Ask your class what school would be like if students were never laughed at for making mistakes.

Hands Together

Goal setting is the activity that is the most important in promoting the condition of spirit of adventure. Students should begin setting goals when they first enter school and continue doing so all the way through high school. Goal-setting skills should be taught and reinforced often. This fun activity is a great way to introduce goal setting to students.

Materials   ▶ Construction paper and markers and pencils

▶ Scissors

▶ Tape

Instructions   1. Have your students think about something they would like to do better on a particular day. Maybe they want to keep their hands to themselves or walk quietly in the hallway.

2. Together, create a class goal, write it on construction paper, and post it prominently in the room.

3. Continue to work on achieving class goals for a few weeks. Make sure the goals are obtainable and that, once they are achieved, they are celebrated by the whole class.

4. Discuss the concept of individual goal setting and proceed as follows:

   First, discuss the topic of goal setting with your students, helping out by providing them with some examples of goals. Ask your students to think about one thing they would like to achieve either personally or academically.

   Next, have the students concentrate on actually setting individual goals. These goals should be obtainable, achievable, measurable, and simple. You may want to give students a few examples of goals, such as raising one's hand before speaking, walking quietly in line, and so forth.

5. Have the students use a pencil to trace around one of their hands on the construction paper and then cut out that portion of the paper that serves as an outline of the hand.

6. Instruct the students to write their goal in the palm of their paper hand. On each of their fingers, have students write what they need to do differently to achieve their goal. For example, in order to walk quietly down the hall, some students may notice that they need to stay in the back of the line or away from their friends.

7. Post the paper hands on the walls of the classroom.

8. At the end of the week, review the students' goals. Recognize and laud the students who are making progress toward their goal.

9. Make sure that students focus on the same goal for several weeks and continue to set goals throughout the school year.

Discussion 1. What was difficult about goal setting?

2. What did it feel like to achieve your goal?

3. What goals would you like to achieve outside of school?

Enrichment Have your students keep goal-setting journals for the entire year so they can keep track not only of their goals but also of their successes and failures.

From time to time throughout the year, give your students specific goal-related writing prompts.

ACTIVITY 3   Let's Play!

Games are a great way for students to experience success and failure and to take risks. In order to promote the condition of spirit of adventure, students need to be exposed to risk-taking opportunities. Students will quickly realize that the rewards of healthy risk taking are many.

Materials

▶ A variety of board games (e.g., Clue, Scrabble, checkers, backgammon) that require decision making

Instructions

1. Tell the class that they are going to have an hour to play board games of their own choosing.
2. Before your students begin play, invite them to take risks that they normally would not, such as leaving an inviting opening for their checkers opponent.
3. After the students have finished playing their games, bring them together for a discussion on risk taking.

Discussion

1. What extra risks did you take while playing your game?
2. Did the risks pay off? Why or why not?
3. In what situations could you take healthier risks? What would the possible outcomes be?

Enrichment

Ask your students to take healthy risks in your classroom. Challenge them to be risk takers every day.

Brainstorm ways students can be smarter risk takers. Certain risks might involve students' raising their hands when they are unsure of an answer or being nice to someone they don't really like.

ACTIVITY 4   My Skills

As they prepare to set goals, students need to be aware of the skills they currently possess. Students should periodically take the time to self-assess and recognize all of their wonderful skills. This activity provides them with a visual reminder that will help them as they begin both to set goals and to take risks to achieve those goals.

Materials
- ▶ Extra-large sheets of butcher paper
- ▶ Markers

Instructions
1. Pair up the students.
2. Give each student a sheet of butcher paper large enough to trace around his or her body. (Partners should help with the tracing.)
3. On the butcher paper, inside the outline of their body, have the students list all the skills they possess, be they academic or social.
4. Invite them to share a few of these skills with their classmates.
5. Ask your students to list, outside the outline of their body, two skills they would like to have.

Discussion
1. What surprised you about your current skills?
2. How can you achieve those skills listed outside the outline of your body?
3. Why is it important for you to take healthy risks?

Enrichment

Have your students write one goal on a slip of paper that has a piece of tape affixed to it so the slip can be taped to something else. Ask them to tape the slip of paper to the butcher paper, positioning it either inside or outside the outline of their body, depending on how close they are to achieving the goal written on the paper. At the end of each week, allow the students to move their goal (the slip of paper) either closer to or farther away from their body. Once the goal is eventually taped inside their body, it is time for them to create new goals.

Activity 5   What Did You Say?

Learning a new skill is a great way for students to take healthy risks. Whether the skill is academic, athletic, or social, students will enjoy learning it. Learning to pronounce and write words from a different language makes this activity especially exciting for the class.

Materials

▶ Audiotapes or CDs of basic words from a different language

▶ A tape player or a CD player

▶ Note cards

▶ Tape

Instructions

1. Introduce your students to a new language by playing language tapes or having a visitor to the classroom teach some words from a different language.

2. On note cards, write several everyday words from the other language and tape the cards to the walls in the classroom. This strategy will help students to become familiar with common words that initially they could not define.

3. Teach your class a few phrases used by speakers of the other language and give the students time to communicate with each other in that language. (Students will also have fun writing their names in a different language.)

4. Introduce your students to several different languages during the school year.

Discussion

1. What is difficult about learning a different language?

2. If you could be fluent in another language, which language would it be and why?

3. Do you think English is a difficult language to learn? Why or why not?

Enrichment

Together with your students, learn American Sign Language (ASL). Learn a few signs each day until the class knows 20 to 30 different words.

ACTIVITY 6   Time Travel

When most people think of positive risk takers, they usually think of explorers, pioneers, inventors, and the like—risk takers with a spirit of adventure. However, one need not do anything grand to qualify as having a spirit of adventure. One must simply be willing to try something new and risk the possibility of failure—as well as the possibility of success.

Materials
- ► Loose-leaf paper and pencils or pens
- ► Loose-leaf notebooks
- ► Crayons

Instructions
1. Tell your students to imagine that they are traveling through time—either in the future or in the past.
2. Have the students create short storybooks about their "adventures."
3. Tell students that, on each page of the storybook, they should draw a picture and write a few words about what life is like in their time period.
4. Have students think about the risks that people had to take in the period they chose.
5. Allow enough time for students to present their stories to the class orally and to show their storybooks.

Discussion
1. What was the biggest risk you took in your time travel?
2. Would you have liked living in the past? Why or why not?
3. What do you think will be different in the future?

Enrichment
Help students build time-travel machines. The machines should be 3-D and contain the 10 most essential items necessary for the trip. Students should be able to explain how their machine works and why they chose the 10 items that they plan to bring with them.

     Teach Your Hobby

It is difficult for someone to take a risk if that person has never been given the opportunity to be a risk taker. For some students, the thought of taking a risk is too intimidating and scary. This activity encourages students to take risks by providing them with a safe and comfortable environment in which to do so.

Materials
▶ None

Instructions
1. Discuss hobbies with your students, making sure that all students get to share their favorite hobby with the class. You may want to get the ball rolling by sharing your favorite hobby with them.
2. Tell the class they are going to prepare a short presentation or demonstration about their hobby. Permit them to bring in props if they want, and be sure to remind them to practice before presenting.
3. Set up a schedule.
4. Remind students that hobby sharing takes place in a No-Laughter zone unless the presenter intends for the audience to laugh.

Discussion
1. What was difficult about presenting in front of the class?
2. Is it easier to present a paper or a hobby? Why?
3. What do you find academically challenging or even a bit scary?

Enrichment
Developing speaking skills is advantageous for students of all ages. Spend some time with your students, working on presentation skills. Invite other teachers or adults into the classroom to listen to the student presentations. If you have access to a camera and a VCR, tape the student presentations so the students can watch themselves at a later date.

ACTIVITY 8　　　　**Meet Someone New**

Taking the time to get to know new people can be a huge risk for students and adults. This activity challenges students to take a risk and get to know somebody new during lunch or recess.

Materials
▶ Small notebooks or notepads and pencils or pens
▶ Sheets of paper with adult names written on them

Instructions
1. Challenge your students to sit with a new student at lunch or to play with someone they haven't played with before during recess.

2. Have them keep a journal about their friend-making experiences, jotting down their impressions in a notebook.

3. Encourage the class to meet students from other grades, as well as any adults in the building besides you.

4. One way to get students to meet adults other than their teacher is to have them go on an autograph hunt with a specific goal in mind:

    Give students a sheet of writing paper on which appear the names of a variety of adults in the school. By the end of the week, students must collect the signatures of every adult whose name appears on the sheet.

Discussion
1. What was the best part about meeting someone new?
2. What was difficult about meeting someone new?
3. Can you recall a time when you felt like an outsider and someone took the time to get to know you?

Enrichment
Together with your students, create a welcoming committee. Those on the welcoming committee should give new students tours of the building, introduce them to others, and be their buddies.

Challenge Activities for Spirit of Adventure

For Students
- ▶ Have students try a new activity that is physical, artistic, or musical in nature. It should involve something they either have never done or have tried unsuccessfully to do.
- ▶ Help students create goals for themselves at home. The goals may have to do with homework, chores, or siblings. Have students keep track of their goals and the progress they make.
- ▶ Encourage students to improve their math skills. Have them do a few especially challenging problems.

For Teachers
- ▶ Set two meaningful professional goals. Make a plan to achieve those goals and stick to it.
- ▶ Challenge yourself to learn something new about teaching. Read a couple of books that are currently being used in graduate education courses. Convince at least one colleague to read the same books.
- ▶ Challenge your colleagues to join you in creating unique lesson plans that involve teachers' taking risks.

CHAPTER SEVEN

LEADERSHIP and RESPONSIBILITY

CONFIDENCE to TAKE ACTION

LEADERSHIP and RESPONSIBILITY

SPIRIT of ADVENTURE

CURIOSITY and CREATIVITY

FUN and EXCITEMENT

SENSE of ACCOMPLISHMENT

HEROES

BELONGING

Activity 1   Our Rules, Our Consequences

In order for students to experience leadership and responsibility, they need to be given the opportunity to make genuine decisions and to experience the consequences of those decisions. For example, students should have a voice in developing rules for the classroom. By allowing them to voice their opinions, you will be fostering their ownership of rules and consequences.

Materials
▶ Writing paper and pencils or pens

Instructions
1. Ask your students to discuss class rules and consequences they have used and experienced in other classes and to disclose which rules worked and which didn't.

2. Tell your students that you would like the class to develop their rules and consequences together.

3. Divide the class into groups of four and give each group a piece of writing paper and pencils.

4. Ask each group to list their major discipline concerns, but make sure they have enough time to discuss the issues.

5. Have each group create three categories or rules that would encompass most of their discipline concerns (e.g., respect each other, be nice, listen).

6. Ask each group to present both their concerns and their three categories to the rest of the class.

7. Have the whole class come to an agreement on three class rules.

8. Mix students into new groups and ask them to think about consequences they should institute for those who break the rules.

9. Gather the students' ideas and put together a plan that works for you and the students.

10. Make sure to revisit the plan and alter it if it is not proving effective.

Discussion
1. Will discipline problems decrease if students create the rules? Explain.

2. Why do we need rules and consequences?

3. What are some rules that everyone—even adults—must live by?

Enrichment
Give students a copy of the school handbook.

Ask for student feedback and ideas concerning the school's discipline policy. Give students the opportunity to present their ideas to the administration.

The New Student Council

Year after year, student council elections prove to be little more than popularity contests. Regardless of whether these popular students are qualified to lead and make decisions, they routinely are elected to represent the student body. This activity challenges students to broaden their horizons by allowing every student to participate in the election process.

Materials
- ▶ 1 slip of paper per student
- ▶ Pencils or pens
- ▶ A box or a bag

Instructions

1. Make sure your students know what the student council is and what council members do. Be very clear about the expectations for student council members. Let your students know that representatives will be chosen on a different basis this year.

2. Ask each student who wishes to be part of the student council to put his or her name on a slip of paper and drop it in a class box or bag.

3. Choose one student to draw student names from the bag. The number of names drawn will depend on how many student council representatives your class is permitted to have.

4. The students whose names are drawn will be your student council representatives for part of the school year. Halfway through the year, choose new student council representatives. Save the other names in the bag and create opportunities for these students to be leaders.

Discussion

1. What does it take to be a good leader?

2. Is it possible for someone be a negative leader?

3. What responsibilities go along with being a school leader?

Enrichment

Ask your class's student council members to keep a journal of their experiences: What decisions have they made? How are meetings run? What roles and responsibilities do they have? If the journals depict little or no authentic decision making, then it is time for the school to restructure its student council.

Chapter 7: Leadership and Responsibility

ACTIVITY 3   You Decide

It is easy to say we want our students to be good decision makers. However, it is difficult to be a good decision maker if you are never given the opportunity to make decisions. On a daily basis, teachers need to create opportunities for students to be decision makers. This activity should help in that respect.

Materials
- You Decide Scenarios
- Note cards
- Writing paper and pencils or pens

Instructions
1. Give your students the You Decide Scenarios and several note cards.
2. Ask your students to be honest and think seriously about what they would do in each decision-making situation and write it on a note card, along with the number that corresponds to the scenario being addressed. Responses can be shared with you and the rest of the class.
3. After your students have had the opportunity to involve themselves in a variety of scenarios, encourage them to list their own real-life decision-making dilemmas. Have them write about certain situations they faced and then let their classmates discuss the options available to them in each instance.

Discussion
1. Why is it difficult to make decisions?
2. How do you make difficult decisions?
3. Whom do you turn to for help when you need it?

Enrichment
Develop a peer mediation system whereby students help each other work through disputes, disagreements, and arguments.

Train students to be peer mediators on the playground or in the hallway. Peer mediators may be distinguishable merely by the words they use. They may also stand out by serving as role models for settling disputes.

You Decide Scenarios

Scenario 1

It is late at night and your favorite TV show is on. You have waited an entire week to watch this show. You just remembered about a big test tomorrow. What do you do? Consider your options and the consequences of each.

Scenario 2

Your best friend overslept and forgot to bring his homework to school. He promises you that he finished his homework last night. He asks to copy yours. If he does not turn in his homework, he says, he will be in big trouble. What do you do? Consider your options and the consequences of each.

Scenario 3

Your sports team is playing a big rival. The last time you played this team, its players were not very nice. Some of your teammates are talking about getting even. What do you do? Consider your options and the consequences of each.

ACTIVITY 4 **Tackling School Issues**

Leaders often must tackle difficult issues. They must make a plan, present it, and then support it by discussing their ideas. This activity helps students practice leadership skills with issues that are important to them.

Materials
► Tackling School Issues Worksheet
► Notebooks and pencils or pens

Instructions
1. Divide your class into groups of four and give each group the Tackling School Issues Worksheet.
2. Have the groups think about several school issues that concern them.
3. Ask students to list the reasons why their group's issues are a concern. Have one student in each group keep track of the group's ideas by writing them on the worksheet.
4. Have students do a short role play (probably in the form of a skit) in front of the class before thinking about a plan of action to deal with one of their concerns.

   For the role play, ask each of the four students to represent one of the following people: a student, an administrator, a teacher, and a parent.

   Encourage the group to think about each person's perspective on the issue they have chosen and to log it in a notebook.
5. Following the role plays, have the groups begin to think about an action plan: How can they go about addressing this problem? With whom do they need to speak? What other information do they need?
6. Be sure to give your students enough time to present their ideas and to follow their action plans.

Discussion
1. What was it like to play the role of the student, administrator, teacher, or parent?
2. Why is it difficult to come to an agreement on issues of concern?
3. How do you solve disputes with your friends?

Enrichment
Take small groups of students on field trips to observe decision-making groups in action (e.g., local activists, the school board, the city council). Make sure to discuss different decision-making styles and formats with your students.

Ask your students if they think teachers generally have a different decision-making style than the individuals and groups they observed.

Tackling School Issues Worksheet

Issue of concern to students

Why issue is of concern

1. _____

1. _____

_____

2. _____

2. _____

_____

3. _____

3. _____

_____

4. _____

4. _____

_____

Raising Student Aspirations: Classroom Activities for Grades K–5
© 2003 by Russell J. Quaglia and Kristine M. Fox. Champaign, IL: Research Press (800) 519-2707

ACTIVITY 5	**Forward or Backward**

Peer pressure, as well as the desire merely to follow the group, often inhibits students' abilities to make decisions. Students need to be given a chance to make decisions regardless of what their peers think or say.

Materials
▶ Blindfolds

Instructions
1. Inform students that, rather than follow what the group does, you want them to make decisions all by themselves.

2. Give each student a blindfold to wear and have everyone line up in the middle of the room. Tell the students that when they agree with a statement, they should take one step forward, and when they disagree, they should take one step backward.

3. Start with a few easy statements, such as "Math is my favorite subject," "School is fun," and "I like recess." Students will easily be able to make up their own minds about these issues.

4. Begin using more complex statements, such as "I treat everyone fairly" or "I feel safe at school" or any other statements that are relevant to you and your class. (Be sure to throw in a few laughter-provoking statements, such as "My teacher is the best.")

5. After the line of students has fallen into disarray, ask students to take off their blindfolds: What do they notice? What does their observation say about decision making? What does it say about the class?

Discussion
1. Was it easy or difficult to make a decision when you did not know what your friends were doing?

2. Did you like making decisions on your own? Explain.

3. When would you rather make a group decision?

Enrichment
Ask students to respond to writing prompts that contain decision-making dilemmas. You may want to choose scenarios that center on certain concerns at your school.

As an alternative to writing, present pictures that depict disagreements or choices to be made. Ask students to interpret the pictures and offer their ideas on how to solve the disagreements.

ACTIVITY 6   Practicing Leadership

Generally speaking, it can be scary and intimidating to take on leadership roles. Thus it is important for students to be given leadership roles in a variety of safe settings. This fun activity allows all students to experience the joys and frustrations of being a leader by assigning them specific roles and responsibilities for group projects.

Materials
▶ Drawing paper and markers
▶ Notepads and pencils or pens

Instructions
1. Choose a group project and assign each group member a specific role. Roles assigned may include listener, note taker, leader, artist, writer, teacher liaison, and so on.
2. Keep in mind that students either love or hate group projects: Rarely are the projects completed by the entire group; more often than not, only a few students in the group end up doing the bulk of the work. The following guidelines should help ensure that everyone in the group stays on task:

   Make sure that each student has a role.

   For each role, furnish several guidelines and responsibilities.

   Remind students that they are not allowed to switch roles and should not take over each other's responsibilities.
3. Keep track of who has what role so that students can play different roles in future projects.

Discussion
1. What was frustrating about being assigned roles?
2. Why was it helpful for some students to have roles but not helpful for others?
3. How can we make sure everyone has a chance to participate in class and group activities?

Enrichment
Together with your students, create classroom jobs. Let each student decide how he or she is going to do the assigned job: Some students may decide that being line leader means to be quiet, whereas others may see it as an opportunity to organize the class and become a vocal leader. Let students discover their own leadership styles and what works best for them.

ACTIVITY 7	**Good Communicators**

Good communication skills are the backbone of good leaders. Leaders need to be able to have their points understood. Any activity, such as this one, that enables students to practice their communication skills promotes the condition of leadership and responsibility.

Materials
- ▶ 8½ × 11–inch sheets of paper bearing different simple designs (one sheet per pair of students)
- ▶ Drawing paper and colored pencils

Instructions
1. Pair up students and give them two sheets of blank paper. Have them sit back-to-back somewhere in the room.
2. Have one student be the describer and the other be the listener.
3. Give each describer a piece of paper with a design on it. The describer's task is to communicate with the listener well enough so that the latter will be able to draw the design that's being described. The rules are as follows:

    The listener cannot talk or look at the design.

    The describer cannot ask questions or look at what is being drawn by the listener.
4. Instruct students to reverse roles. Have them trade designs with other pairs so that the new describer has a fresh design to communicate.
5. Let students compare their designs. After everyone has had a chance to participate, ask for student feedback: What was difficult? How can we become better communicators? How can we become better listeners?
6. Give the students more intricate and challenging designs and let them try communicating again.

Discussion
1. Is it easier to be the describer or the listener? Explain.
2. Why is it important to be a good communicator?
3. How can we become better listeners?

Enrichment
Play a game of charades with your students, making them communicate through body language instead of through talk. This activity helps students learn to be better communicators by forcing them to use a different, more difficult method of communicating.

Perhaps one of the most difficult skills for students of all ages to master is the art of listening. Like other skills, listening skills need to be practiced.

Materials   ▶ A variety of listening games (e.g., Telephone, Red Light/Green Light, Simon Says)

Instructions   1. In order to practice listening skills, take the time to play a listening game once a week. Begin with a fun game of Simon Says.

2. To start the game, give a series of instructions. Students should follow your instructions only if you say, "Simon says," prior to giving the instructions.

   For example, you might say, "Simon says, 'Jump up and down.'" In that case, the students should jump. However, you might also say, simply, "Sit down." In that case, anyone who sits down is immediately disqualified. The reason? You didn't preface your instruction with "Simon says."

   Instruct those students who have been eliminated to watch and listen as the others finish the game.

3. At the end of each game, give out several listening rewards to the students who tried their best to listen.

Discussion   1. What makes someone a good listener?
2. Why do leaders need to be good listeners?
3. What distracts you from being a good listener?

Enrichment   Ask students to listen as you read a short story or even just a paragraph. Inform your students that at the end of the story you will be asking several questions. The good listeners will be able to answer the questions.

Challenge Activities for Leadership and Responsibility

For Students
- ► Have students take a stance on an issue they feel strongly about. Tell them not to follow the popular choice if it is not one they believe in.
- ► Encourage students to become leaders on the playground. Remind them to play games according to the rules and not to get involved in disputes.
- ► Have students create their own action plan to be a better leader. Encourage them to think of ways they can take on more responsibility both at school and at home.

For Teachers
- ► Question the status quo and the way things have always been done. Be an educational leader and promote an agenda you believe in.
- ► Teach leadership skills to all students every day. Document student progress.
- ► Be a positive leader in your school. Don't allow negative talk and attitudes to set the tone for the school.
- ► Support student initiatives and ideas. Create opportunities for student voices to be heard.

CHAPTER EIGHT

CONFIDENCE to TAKE ACTION

CONFIDENCE to TAKE ACTION

LEADERSHIP and RESPONSIBILITY

SPIRIT of ADVENTURE

CURIOSITY and CREATIVITY

FUN and EXCITEMENT

SENSE of ACCOMPLISHMENT

HEROES

BELONGING

ACTIVITY 1   My Strengths

Students who exhibit the necessary confidence to take action are aware of their strengths and try to correct their weaknesses. As this activity shows, it is important for all students to understand their strengths and how those strengths add to the success of the class.

Materials
- ► Sentence Starters Worksheet
- ► Writing paper and pencils or pens

Instructions
1. Give the Sentence Starters Worksheet to your students and instruct them to complete each sentence. (You can either use the worksheet provided in this section or devise one that better suits your needs.)
2. Collect the worksheets after the students have completed them.
3. Read a few of the completed sentences from each worksheet and see if the class can decide whose worksheet you are reading.
4. Ask the students to give themselves a round of applause for all the things they are good at doing.

Discussion
1. How do you get good at doing something?
2. What would you like to do better?
3. What is a strength you see in one of your classmates?

Enrichment
Ask students to list all of their skills and to jot down after each one whether they are OK, good, or great at performing the skill. You may have to create a common skill sheet for everyone to use. After students fill out the sheet, discuss with them how their skills can help the entire class.

Sentence Starters Worksheet

1. I am OK at _____.

2. I am good at _____.

3. I am great at _____.

4. I work really hard at _____.

5. I am a good friend because _____.

6. I love doing _____.

7. I like it when people ask my advice about _____.

8. I enjoy helping others at _____.

9. I think the reason I am loyal is _____.

10. I would love to learn how to _____.

Raising Student Aspirations: Classroom Activities for Grades K–5
© 2003 by Russell J. Quaglia and Kristine M. Fox. Champaign, IL: Research Press (800) 519-2707

ACTIVITY 2   **What I Like about You**

It is always nice when students hear compliments from their class-mates. Unfortunately, some students think their classmates don't like them simply because the classmates either did not ask them to play or said something that was not so nice. This activity encourages students to build each other's confidence by sharing each other's strengths.

Materials   ► Enough marbles so that two students can have in their possession the same-colored marble at the same time (e.g., two yellow marbles, two blue, two red)

► A CD player and assorted CDs

Instructions 1. Have the students sit in a circle and give each one a marble.

2. Tell them that you will be playing music, and that, as the music plays, they are to continue passing one marble at a time to the classmate sitting to their right.

3. Tell the students that, once the music stops, they are to quit passing marbles, stand up, find the student who is holding the same-colored marble, and sit next to him or her.

4. Have the students say something nice about the student they are now sitting next to, pointing out one of their classmate's strengths.

5. Continue this activity for several rounds.

Discussion   1. What did it feel like to have something nice said about you?

2. How can we be nicer to each other every day?

3. What is the nicest thing someone has ever done for you?

Enrichment   As a class, create a huge banner detailing all the nice things the students do. Students should be allowed to color, paint, or draw on the banner. Everyone should help think of a fun and creative title.

It is a challenge for students of all ages to understand their emotions. Students may be in a bad mood and not know why, or they may feel good and not really know why. This charades activity helps students recognize their different moods.

Materials   ► Mood Cards (one card per student)

Instructions   1. Stack the Mood Cards facedown in a pile.

2. Tell the class that they are going to play mood charades. (Depending on the size of your class, you may want to divide the class in half.)

3. Have students pick a Mood Card and act out the mood without talking. Classmates should try to identify the mood.

4. After this activity has been completed, ask your students to describe a time when they were in one of the moods on the cards. Make sure you give each student an opportunity to share a mood story.

Discussion   1. Why do our moods change?

2. How can your classmates help you out of a bad mood?

3. What is your favorite mood?

Enrichment   Ask students to keep a mood journal. On the first page of the journal there should be a list of possible moods. Each day, students should pick the mood they have been in most of the day and explain why they have been feeling this way. After a few weeks, collect and discuss the mood journals.

Mood Cards

Depressed	**Happy**
Sad	**Angry**
Mad	**Excited**
Optimistic	**Pessimistic**
Eager	**Anxious**
Hopeful	**Alert**
Lazy	**Energetic**

ACTIVITY 4　　　For a Cause

Although it is easy to care about different causes, it is often quite a challenge to become involved and do something about them. This activity allows students to work toward making a difference in their community.

Materials　▶ Specific to the fund-raising method chosen

Instructions
1. Let your students know that you would like the class to raise money for a cause of the students' choosing.

2. Spend some time discussing causes the students believe in and how the class can help these causes.

3. Together with your students, think of ways to earn money for a special cause (e.g., a bake sale, a penny drive, a read-a-thon).

4. Once the students have decided on one cause, have them get started. Make sure all the students become involved in the project.

Discussion
1. What does it feel like to get involved?

2. How did the people you were helping react to your efforts?

3. What skills did you learn by doing this activity?

Enrichment　Organize a schoolwide business day for which classes are to make something to sell. These items may include baked goods, toys, or artwork. Proceeds from the business day should go toward something the school needs.

ACTIVITY 5   Confident Person

Students have certain, varied notions of what a confident person looks like. Unfortunately, students often do not see themselves as confident people. This activity encourages students to look at all the wonderful attributes they have.

Materials
- ▶ Drawing paper and colored pencils
- ▶ Scissors

Instructions

1. Let students know that they are going to create new super-heroes—themselves.

2. Have students create several drawings that depict their best assets in an exaggerated fashion. For example, if someone is a good listener, he or she might draw a huge ear.

3. Ask the students to name their superheroes and be able to explain their drawings.

4. Have students cut out the drawings of these superheroes and post them on the walls of the classroom.

Discussion

1. What makes a superhero?

2. What flaws do superheroes have?

3. If you could have one special talent or skill, what would it be? Why?

Enrichment

Ask students to create a cartoon strip with their superhero as the protagonist. What does their superhero do that is so wonderful? Remember that the superheroes should possess realistic traits.

The Letter

This activity, which gives students an opportunity to write a letter to their next year's teacher, is a great one to save till the end of the school year. It serves as an effective confidence booster because it enables students to see how well they have developed during the year.

Materials
▶ Tracking Learning and Skills Worksheet
▶ Writing paper and pencils or pens

Instructions
1. Ask your students to think about what they have learned this year. Give them the Tracking Learning and Skills Worksheet to help them keep track of their scholastic achievements, their strengths, and their social skills.

2. Tell your students that they are going to write a letter to next year's teacher. The letter should be an "all about me" letter. Make sure students include what they hope to learn next year, as well as their concerns about the next grade. (For students who are not yet readers, encourage them to draw pictures of things they like, or get their parents to help them write their letters.)

3. Prior to the end of the school year, visit the students' new classrooms for the following year and give their future teachers the letters.

Discussion
1. What is the hardest thing you learned this year?
2. What do you hope to learn next year?
3. What is your biggest concern for next year?

Enrichment
Ask students to write letters of thanks to the people who have helped them throughout the school year. These people may include custodians or secretaries or even their parents.

Tracking Learning and Skills Worksheet

What I learned this year

1. _____

2. _____

3. _____

4. _____

5. _____

6. _____

7. _____

8. _____

9. _____

10. _____

My strengths and social skills

1. _____

2. _____

3. _____

4. _____

5. _____

6. _____

7. _____

8. _____

9. _____

10. _____

For many students, having friends is an important component of self-confidence. This activity is fun, and it helps celebrate the importance of friendship.

Materials
► Magazines
► Drawing paper and markers
► Glue
► Scissors

Instructions
1. Ask your students to think about their friends: Why are they friends? What fun things do they do together? What is special about their friends?

2. Have them find pictures or drawings that represent their friendships and create a collage—a friendship collage—from these pictures.

3. Encourage students to share their collages with the class. It does not matter who their friends are. What is important is that students recognize the importance of friendship.

Discussion
1. Why is it important to have friends?

2. What do you do when you and your friends disagree?

3. How can you make new friends?

Enrichment
Depending on the age of your students, choose a book about friendship to read to the class. The book might be about kids who have animals or siblings as their friends. You may even decide to read an adventure book about two friends.

ACTIVITY 8   Encouraging Words

We all like to hear words of encouragement. Words can be powerful and have a strong effect on one's confidence. This activity helps students understand the power of the words they use.

Materials
- ► Note cards
- ► Tape or thumbtacks

Instructions
1. Have your students start thinking about words with opposite meanings, such as *good/bad, pretty/ugly, smart/stupid.*
2. Ask them what it feels like when someone calls them a good name or offers words of encouragement, such as "Good job" or "Hang in there."
3. Ask them what it feels like when someone calls them a bad name or discourages them by saying such negative things as "Bad job" or "You're stupid."
4. Tell your students that your classroom is one that, from now on, will use words of encouragement. That way, students and teachers alike will enter the room with the understanding that put-downs are not allowed.
5. Ask students to think of words of encouragement or positive phrases and then write them on the note cards. Because the note cards will be taped or tacked to one of the walls, the students should be reminded that they must make sure the words are legible and dark enough to be seen from a distance.
6. Remind your students that when they are not sure what to say in certain situations, they should look at the wall where the words of encouragement are posted.

Discussion
1. What does it feel like to receive a compliment?
2. What is the nicest compliment you ever received?
3. Why do you think kids say mean things to each other?

Enrichment
Ask your students to follow the "no put-down" rule on the playground as well.

When students get angry, help them to seek another solution. You may even want to develop a peer mediation program with your students.

Challenge Activities for Confidence to Take Action

For Students
- ► Have students congratulate themselves whenever they successfully complete a school project.
- ► Have your students take on an assignment that may seem a bit challenging. Have them learn the more difficult spelling words, participate in a science fair, or write an extra story.
- ► Tell your students not to let others take advantage of them. Encourage them to let others know how they feel.

For Teachers
- ► Assert your ideas and opinions on a matter pertaining to academics. Convince your colleagues to listen and try your ideas.
- ► Take the time to recognize all the skills you bring to your profession.
- ► Compliment your colleagues on the hard work they do every day. Write anonymous notes of encouragement and praise to colleagues and students.

About the Authors

Russell J. Quaglia, Ed.D., is the executive director of the Global Institute for Student Aspirations at Endicott College in Beverly, Massachusetts, and a professor of education. During an appearance on NBC TV's *Today Show,* he was described as America's foremost authority on the development and achievement of student aspirations.

A dynamic speaker, Dr. Quaglia travels extensively, presenting research-based information on student aspirations and motivation to audiences throughout the United States and around the world.

His opinions and comments on aspirations and controversial educational topics have been much sought after and published in national media such as the *Washington Post, Boston Globe, New York Times, USA Today, Chronicle of Higher Education,* and *Education Week.* He also has appeared on CNN and C-SPAN.

He received his bachelor's degree from Assumption College in Worcester, Massachusetts; a master of arts degree in economics from Boston College; and a master of education and doctorate from Columbia University, specializing in the area of organizational theory and behavior. Dr. Quaglia's research has been published in numerous professional journals, including *Research in Rural Education, Educational Administration Quarterly, Journal of Instructional Psychology, American School Board Journal, Adolescence,* and *Journal of Psychological and Educational Measurement.* His thoughts and opinions have also appeared in popular magazines such as *Reader's Digest, Better Homes and Gardens, Parent and Family,* and *Ladies' Home Journal.*

Kristine M. Fox is the director of field services for the Global Institute for Student Aspirations and an instructor at Endicott College. Most of her work involves teaching the importance of student aspirations to administrators, teachers, and students in schools throughout North America and abroad. In addition to working with these groups, she discusses with parents and other community members the significance of student aspirations.

She has presented extensively at conferences and workshops. She has conducted her site work throughout New England and also at a number of disparate locales such as Alaska, Arizona, Mexico, Toronto, and England.

She received her bachelor's degree from the University of Michigan and a master's degree in education from Harvard University. She has experience both as a classroom teacher and as a school administrator.